The Seasons of Yes

The Seasons of Yes

Poems by

Lorraine Schechter

SANTA FE

© 2007 by Lorraine Schechter. All rights reserved.

No part of this book may be reproduced in any form or by any electronic or mechanical means including information storage and retrieval systems without permission in writing from the publisher, except by a reviewer who may quote brief passages in a review.

Sunstone books may be purchased for educational, business, or sales promotional use. For information please write: Special Markets Department, Sunstone Press, P.O. Box 2321, Santa Fe, New Mexico 87504-2321.

Library of Congress Cataloging-in-Publication Data

Schechter, Lorraine, 1945-
  The seasons of yes : poems / by Lorraine Schechter.
    p. cm.
  ISBN 978-0-86534-602-4 (pbk. collector's edition: alk. paper)
  ISBN 978-0-86534-607-9 (pbk. : alk. paper)
  1. Seasons--Poetry. I. Title.

PS3619.C337S43 2008
811'.6--dc22
                                      2007024549

WWW.SUNSTONEPRESS.COM
SUNSTONE PRESS / POST OFFICE BOX 2321 / SANTA FE, NM 87504-2321 /USA
(505) 988-4418 / ORDERS ONLY (800) 243-5644 / FAX (505) 988-1025

*For my family, friends, teachers, and students…
and this most beautiful Earth we share*

Contents

Introduction / 10

Spring / 12

    Gifts / 14
    Baptism by Waterfall / 15
    The Poetry Teacher / 16
    11:11 / 17
    Full of Leisure / 18
    Ode to Pencil / 20
    About Silence / 22
    In Memoriam / 23
    Passover / 24
    Long View / 25
    The geography of my childhood / 26
    Pantoum for Spring / 27

Summer / 28

    Sunday morning, early / 30
    Her Own Nature / 32
    A Day at *Le Caire* / 33
    A discordant sound 34
    A Rainbow for Gravity / 35
    Chupadero, Summer 1999 / 36
    There is a heart below this heart / 37
    Jones Beach, N.Y. 1952 / 38
    Monterey Drive / 39
    Song of the Conejos / 40
    View From the Studio / 41
    The Twins / 42
    Sun Cycle / 44
    On a hot summer's night / 45
    Woman in Yellow / 46
    Retreat: A Day on Lama Mountain / 48

Fall / 52

    In praise of / 54
    Ghost Ranch / 55
    In La Cienega / 56
    Love creates havoc out of nothing / 58
    At SITE Santa Fe in November / 59
    Retreat at Mountain Cloud / 60
    Lament for Rusty / 61
    In the Shadow of the Master / 62
    The Magic of Making / 63
    Weir Farm Fragments / 64
    Calder's Universe / 66
    Just Before Fall Equinox / 67

Winter / 68

    Winter in Tesuque / 70
    Don't Believe Them / 71
    Rousseau's War. 1894 / 72
    The Man from Lodz / 73
    Two Poems at Full Moon: New Year, 1999 / 74
    Love / 76
    Midwinter / 77
    Missing Verneer / 78
    What He Didn't See / 80
    February 2nd / 81
    I Didn't Have a *Bas Mitzvah* / 82
    Chupadero, January 2000 / 84
    Black Painting / 85

Spring, Again / 86

    What do you plan to do? / 89

Acknowledgments / 91

 # Introduction

Like the seasons, my poetry writing comes in cycles. This collection of poems comes from a six-year period when the need to write was as urgent as the need for water or food. I wrote almost daily, much of the time in my journal, but also in the language of rhythm and image joined with the pleasure in word and sound that said "poem." The themes are those of a woman at mid-life and reveal my passions: art and nature, family and friends, meditation and yoga. Also like the seasons, the poems offer a rich range of moods, colors and textures—what was dark becomes light, what was active becomes still, what was empty becomes full—and back again.

This life of change and our journey of becoming are two of the most compelling motivations for both my poems and visual art. Poetry and art help me to observe and note what is happening. When I'm lucky they surprise me, revealing deeper truths before my conscious mind is aware. But the primary impetus of all my work is the inner vision and voice that has guided me for as long as I can remember, and the process of creating I call giving form to spirit.

But why Yes? Several years ago I made a drawing that changed my life. Looking for the theme for my next body of work, I began playing with calligraphic marks. These evolved into the word yes. I repeated it in a different style, then in another color. Soon the whole page was filled with a rainbow of dancing yes-es and I continued to the next page, and the next. In that stunning and magical moment the conceptual basis for a project I subsequently called "The Book of Yes: An Artist's Answer to No" was born.

I made a one-year commitment to work on the images daily. Each one would be the same size, and had to include the word yes as either the structure of the design, as a calligraphic mark, or to create texture and text. With each "page" I would experiment and try something new to keep myself on my own growing edge. Fourteen months and 378 mixed media paintings later, the strength of my affirmation filled the Santuario de Guadalupe in Santa Fe where I held an exhibition of these works.

"The Book of Yes: An Artist's Answer to No" is a visual journal of my quest to find meaning and beauty in my life. The poems in *The Seasons of Yes* share the same odyssey, though in a less structured, more organic manner. Most were written while I worked on the paintings, and are expressive of a particular time of the year in either tone or image; they share a similar life affirming vision. This interweaving of art and poetry can be seen on my web site (www.lorraineschechter.com) in a suite of twelve prints also called The Seasons of Yes.

I leave you with my poems and the hope that they bring you pleasure, inspiration, and the possibility of yes even as a torrent of "no's" assails us.

—Lorraine Schechter
Santa Fe, New Mexico

Spring

Gifts

a Sung landscape, mountains
extending into stillness
broken by the light tremolo
of a lark on a branch
drawn with a single stroke,

a house filled with roses
yellow dipped in the same sunset
as the Sangre de Cristos,

mums so opulent, their spidery reach
makes nests for hovering butterflies,
bees painted yellow with nectar,

pansies, the color of cream
the orange of dried blood ready to plant
inviting the garden into full bloom,

a celadon cup, the throaty
music of Nina Simone, ripe
strawberries hand dipped in white,
then dark chocolate, its drip
caught in the drying.

Tu Fu said *a good rain knows its season*—
a photograph of the first buds
of Spring wet with rain.

Baptism By Waterfall

Water pounding on rock
deafening
roaring the name of God
into every rivulet.

The smell of damp
inhabiting bones
rocks slippery with algae
small plants in crevices
where stone has turned to earth
absorbed a seed
and bloomed
while God said
Listen, life is here
this moment.

The Poetry Teacher

for Jay Udall

The mystery of words to mean
more than they say, the gift
of clear vision, lessons in the subtlety
of language, teachings on the blessings
of words—he shakes his head
flinging back a lock of hair
and the vibrato of his voice
catches in the back of his throat
and in mine, as his pictures
painted large with fine detail
move across landscapes of a heart
grown vast with the specifics of love.

Good, he says, surprising—
I'm caught off guard not expecting
to be seen—his ear hearing
beyond words behind words
through words into worlds
where silence speaks pages.

11:11

spiral patterns on the table
the pressure of pencil (yellow) on paper (white)
fly buzzing on the window
I think, should I pull out the swatter
grasshopper hops in the door
small plane drones overhead
cat rubs my leg, his signal for attention
smell of petunias floats on the breeze
other cat chomps her food
neighbor's dog barks, then growls
car scatters gravel turning in the driveway
radio pounding rap
the plane again

it's 11:12

Full of Leisure

plum blossoms open
clouds expand.
I hear spring
in the wind.

Spring, birth season
the year
just beginning.

Across time and space
  a square window
    mesh covered red chimneys
      blue sky and white clouds
a long *kakemono*
  silk, paper and gold
    teal blue and cream
      the sign for long life
a celebration of today.

Full of leisure
plum blossoms awaken
early,
mind emptying itself.

Sliding on straw mats
in sunlight,
      then shadow
a fresh green leaf—
tea bowl smell scenting air.

Emptiness
filled with spirit
a moment of bliss
whisper of wind.

Full of leisure
sipping tea with friends—
aah!

(A collective poem by Kate Besser, Sue Sturtevant, Gretchen Garner, Noel Hudson, Sakina, and Lorraine Schechter, who took the liberty to do some editing.)

Ode to Pencil

I   No computer can replace
       the feel of you in my hand,
       your weight
       and the pressure of fingers
       along your hexagonal edges,
       the shape of the indentation
       you leave
       on the pad of my middle finger.

II   We grew up together
       you and I,
       and you became an extension
       of all I think,
               when I write,
       and all I see,
               when I draw,
       and do
           as I chew on you
       wondering,
               what next?

III   How many of you
       have I known intimately?
       Eberhard Faber,
       Berol Ensign,
       Blackhawk and Ebony,
                     Eagle Turquoise.
       My favorite being a 2.5
       the right hardness of graphite
       to glide
       on a smooth paper's surface
       and erase
       clean,
       your pink-topped hat
       compressed into ferrule
       secure for countless rubbings
       until gone.
       I run the risk then
       of abrasion
       your mettalic edge
       ripping through.

IV   You taught me
about yellow,
a warm protective coat
for a crystalline leaded
core.
How many times have I sat
chipping off your paint
in long splinters of color,
fingernail
carving into your soft warmth
initials
and designs?

V   Designing,
you are irreplaceable,
the touch of you on paper
a flowing set of marks
across time in space
forming worlds.
I love to form words
              with you in my hand.
And the words move
into action
through your presence on the page.

VI   We're old friends
you and I.
I learned to write with you,
making my letters
just so
until I reinvented my signature,
learning to draw.

Holding you I feel secure,
a known land
of unlimited potential
when all else fails.

About Silence

How do I write about silence?
How do I write a poem
when the stillness pervades
and no thought catches
the mind's eye?
How do I write about
descending into deep peace?

Do I talk
about the endless cobalt
of the morning
just before the sun
rises over the Sangres?
Or the way the cat
fits herself across my chest
paws draped over my shoulders like a shawl?
Do I speak of the no-sound
when the refrigerator stops humming?

Silence, the science of stillness
when I and thou
and naming
become irrelevant.

In Memoriam

for Dick Lukosius

The teacher taught more
than he knew, opening
mind windows uncurtained
seeing beyond knowns. He laughed
short sharp barks
releasing the weight of a heart
too hurt to know the beauty of blue.

Hands arcing he shaped color
texture into a vessel brimming
with luminous space
space breathing the light of his passion.
You can too, he said, a diamond
reflecting facets of infinite possibility
when all the world was draped in black.

Storytelling, beachwalking
wavewatching he taught
the lesson of the moon from new to full
in only twenty eight days, the feminine
before it was politically correct.
And one young woman afraid to be
grew into all she was and more.

Passover

Like my ancestors five thousand years ago
fighting Pharaoh's rule
this beating heart
caged in anger, grief, desire
longs for liberation
seeing its enemy
locked in the mirror.

Long View

for Mara Whitridge

Below me a party of clouds
below them scraggled shadows
showering the landscape

in the distance a horizon
as if standing at the edge of the Atlantic
eyes riding the latitude to Spain.

I painted this horizon once.
I captured it as if picking
an endangered wild iris; now

looking out to sea across miles
of iridescent green a pelican,
a heron, a grebe in the foam

join us as we comb the beach
gathering shells, salty gifts
to pocket for home. The dog darts down

to water's edge snapping at waves
her footprints and ours a sandpainting
washed clean by tide slapping shore.

The geography of my childhood

was limited to four white walls
a Good and Plenty floor of linoleum
black and white and lavender nursery rhymes.
I was stuck with Jack and Jill
up and down, up and down
a treadmill that had no end. One day

I collected a favorite doll
my crayons and a pad.
I packed them in my tiny red
Cinderella suitcase
and at five years old
ran away from home
for the first time, escaping
to the roof of our five story apartment house
where I could see the world
and imagine freedom I didn't know.

Pantoum for Spring

We walk searching for images
the sound of earth moving
well worn paths
voices calling, questioning, laughing

The sound of earth moving
a lizard scampers across my feet
voices calling, questioning, laughing
air heavy with pollen

A lizard scampers across my feet
Spring like just-washed hair
air heavy with pollen
the sun's heat warming belly and breasts

Spring like just-washed hair
pink plum blossoms, light green buds
the sun's heat warming belly and breasts
birds gathering, chattering in silver trees

Pink plum blossoms, light green buds
well worn paths
birds gathering, chattering in silver trees
we walk searching for images

we walk seeking visions.

Summer

Sunday morning, early

the last sliver of moon says listen—
in this moment life is born;
the neighbors still dream
of winning the lottery
or something darker.
The cat returns with a mouse
squirming between his white incisors
cutting into flesh. I could hear
the tearing if I listened,

the cherry tree so fat with fruit
the branches drip
inviting first one bird
then another to taste.
The second cat, grey stripes flashing,
flies up the tree licking lips
I'd just noticed were delicate pink.

Under the grapevines
a bright orange globe
peeks over the horizon
and what was colorless is now
a thousand shades of green
the veined wonder called grape leaf
holding the light
rolling it across her vast
exquisitely shaped expanse
hiding plump clusters.

Hummingbirds hover at their red nectars—
scarlet runner beans, trumpet vines
a feeder with red dye
like a hooker in her red dress.

I listen for words to color
the extreme whiteness of the page
washed in the sounds of a fresh morning
a dog barks, a car revs its engine,
neighbors make love
and the emptiness
that isn't blank
is filled.

Her Own Nature

My camp counselor gave me permission.
A city girl in the wild, I ran
to the studio, pulled open the drawer
scissors, paper and glue, wire and string
a rainbow of color spread in an arc,
and closed the door to outside.

Three shapes shifted in space
the balance a delicate dance
of weight against weight
playing out string on wire
until the whole steadied but just
for a moment, the breeze
inviting the next *pas de trois*.
seahorses riding on air.

Across the studio floor
bits of colored paper
scattered like leaves.

A Day at *Le Caire*

for Christopher Clapp

Crill soup with dill
artichaut vinaigrette
on the cusp of a perfect day
we lunched outside
        in a whole other lifetime—
where cuckoos and nightingales sang, the trail
edged with lavender and wild thyme,
as we climbed to the saddle
              a mountain throne with a world view
the Alps, white capped to the North,
below
        to the South,
                  the Mediterranean
diamond light striking azure surface,
your body heaven,
wordless against mine.

A discordant sound

cricket-like but more insistent
wakes me at eleven p.m. and continues
with precision, at exact intervals
one minute long. It's mechanical cry
sharp edged, cuts through the night
into my sleep, a mother responding
to a call of distress: the fire alert
alerting the world of a dying
battery; chirp again.

Helpless, stuck on the wall
at ten feet up, it wants attention.
Ladderless, I'm stuck below
limited to a table, a stepladder
out of reach at eight feet.
It's going to be a long night.

Between each cry is 59 seconds
of quiet, the night's stillness
broken by a dog's bark, the whirr
of traffic on the highway, an occasional acceleration.
In 59 seconds universes are built and collapse.

I recall a discussion from the day.
A friend asked, "How do you tell the difference
between a real and a fake diamond?" and answered
"The fake diamond is perfect."

Outside the real crickets begin again
their melodic chirping
softer, louder, high-pitched
the tall grasses vibrating with their dialogue.

In the space of sixty minutes,
I can go to Walmart's and buy new batteries,
borrow a ladder and replace that fake cricket,
perfect in its metronomic tyranny

A Rainbow for Gravity

My secret garden is swathed
in dangling particles, grape vines and
hot red flowers trumpeting
a fanfare for hummers. In all this racket
I chew my words
        as a meat grinder masticates chuck, or
        a washing machine devours errant socks,
and invite the participles to join in the feast.

Under the arbor of language, I
collage two and three words into cogency,
cadences more like Sophie Tucker than the Supremes,
who could take two or three words
repeat them seven or eight times
with enough beat and amplification
to keep us dancing for hours. Kegs of beer
and fat joints made everything sound good.

But that was the sixties,
and so am I,
words shipwrecked on seas of forgetfulness.
Gravity tells all.

Chupadero , Summer 1999

I
Sweat drops tickling
reddened face streaked
climbing rock to rock
cool river running faster…
a waterfall! Oooh!

Noonday heat melting
rocks on the mesa
a pinon's shadow
absorbing sweat in the dark
suddenly a shower…cool.

Dragonfly, humming-
bird hovers in the rain
a coyote
crosses my path at sunset
all day on the cushion.

II
Clock striking twelve noon
dog howling in delight
singing in time.

Fat wet drops of rain
fall unfelt by a body
waterfall soaked.

Cool summer rain falls
parched arroyo—suddenly
runs fast—no crossing.

Old friend falters
losing sense of balance.
I cry out. He laughs.

There is a heart below this heart

as if lignite
turned in
on itself.

At its center,
at the absolute center,
a fossil

the delicate pattern
of a fern,
which unfurled

could crack the stone
breaking it down
into sand

as a dandelion can
penetrating Harlem pavement
in the heat of summer.

Jones Beach, N.Y. 1952

Dad called me "waterbug"
all day at the beach riding the waves
beside him, holding hands
fingers shriveled, lips turned blue.

Sliced egg sandwiches with salt from the sea
sand gritty in teeth and crotch, we sat
under a striped umbrella in a circle of shade
a touch and go haven with Mom.

My brother and I built castles, huge forts
shaped with our tin pail mold, feathers
for flags and driftwood fences,
sturdy walls of shell.

At the ocean's edge I hunted for bubbles
digging madly for tiny crabs; watching
late in the day as the water rose
filling our moat, castles and village invaded.

We swam on the incoming tide
bodies red as sunset
Dad at my side riding the waves
fingers shriveled, lips turned blue.

Monterey Drive

for Sue Sturtevent

Oncoming night, the dogs begin a round of song
body dripping with fatigue
airless, not a breath–but the birds don't notice
a cottonwood ten feet around spreads its rustle.

Body dripping with fatigue
I open the door to the impending dark
a cottonwood ten feet around spreads its rustle
the empty garden wide in its bareness.

I open the door to the impending dark
finally a breeze
the empty garden wide in its bareness
and two young girls swing their legs in the moonlight.

Finally a breeze
neighbors' soft Spanish voices
two young girls swing their legs in the moonlight
a woman writes at her table bathed in light.

Neighbors' soft Spanish voices
oncoming night, the dogs begin a round of song
a woman writes at her table bathed in light
airless, not a breath but the birds don't notice.

Song of the Conejos

At 5 a.m. the river sings
and only silence
to hear
my breath a white cloud
in the cold.
In this moment, stillness
stillness so wide
a whole army could move through it
and know peace.

Slowly, slowly
the dark turns to day
and one then another bird sings
in the tree next to my tent
confusing its blue
with the sky.

View From the Studio

all day the hummingbirds flitted and fought
and fed on sugared water; the cat caught two

locust trees with shaggy manes along their trunks
called junk trees lasting only fifteen years

Russian sage with lavender flowers, purple penstemon
magenta hollyhocks, a pathway to the ultraviolet

yellow ice flowers banding the border
a final glint of brightness as

the grey leaves of the Russian olive match the sky
one dancing, the other loaded with clouds

the studio is whipped by wind, a poem flies
across the room, words sail in mid-air

The Twins

Ranny lifted her head
lips parted like a slice of orange
and sang an old tune
May the longtime sunshine…

Hart smiled, robed in clover
       hands overhead
       like flying cranes
and danced, the two
like the rings of Saturn

Hart's laugh glittering silver
       Ranny's glissandos goldfish
       breaking the surface of a pond
green with summer.

If Einstein asked them
Is the universe friendly?
       Why yes! Ranny
       would point to the Earth
       to the chocolate Lab eager at her side
       to the stream as it reappeared
       beyond the orchard.

Hart noticed the rainbow light
where stream became waterfall,
yes.
She sat cat curled around
her neck, tail an elegant question,
yes.

The sisters saw each other
in reverse
        constellations of eyes
        nose mouth and chin
        clustered in a sky
        blushing pink
but distinct
like Mars from Venus.

Sun Cycle

House bathed in indigo, moon riveting shadows
each step a blind blessing into day.

A hot shower unties muscles
roped to dreams of flying, falling spread eagled.

One round yolk sits nested in its white
soaking rye toasted umber.

Metta, sixteen pounds stretched in the sun
his hair electric, brushed handsome.

I swim in Azo yellow, rice paper spirals—
an effulgence of images drenches the studio.

Fed by the etched curves of a halved cabbage
purple pattern and design tastier than lunch.

How do I teach my student to paint space
as he does the pear, its shadow?

Walking the arroyo home: fossilized sea shells
smell of ocean encircling a prehistoric globe.

Smell of chicken basted with tamari, ginger
red coals invite me into my neighbor's yard.

We watch the sky, its sunset dance
color turning, releasing into night.

I quickly turn the pages of P. D. James
eyes insisted open for the ending.

On a hot summer's night

I forgot how to sleep;
bed became prison
        restless images banging
        on bars of sleepless eyes
in the darkness cat snores
        muffled by the heat
        and Daniel's voice
describing jungles soaked in steam
villages piled high with bodies, parts…
        the helpless flutter of his hand
        sweat falling in streams
bleeding half moons
under his arms.

Dog barks build in ferocity
answering each other at three a.m.
        curtains slap windows
        and rivers of fear
pour through channels
of drenched sheets.

Cats hide from the smell of ozone
        filling the room acid yellow
        with the first strike of lightning
rain slashing through screens
        and the hanging leaves on a collage
        circle in the wind
thin blue edges startling
the blackground.

Woman in Yellow

> *The artist and poet possess an interior light*
> *which transforms objects to make a new world of them.*
> —Henri Matisse

She sits in a rainbow of color
her hands folded in her lap
like plump flowers
        shaped like the bows in her dress
        or butterflies lifting precariously
in the Mistral
        wind entering through shutters
        lining the light of the azure sea
and just a glimpse of a horizon
as if you could see to Sardinia.

She sits in her yellow
        like linden flowers
        delicate, slightly green.
Matisse filled each section
with layers of color, yellow merging
into blue green violet
in the light of Nice on a hot afternoon.

She sits under the green brim
of her hat cooled
        but oh the electric red of the tiles
        at her feet
with a flick of his brush
        the pattern in outline
        as are fingers and lifted eyebrows
        thin nose
strong chin, necklace
not quite circling her neck.

He loved space
        he loved women
        but he loved color more
and the shapes color filled
and the space where shapes
        breathed
        open
his line just a gesture:
        one edge and the other
        like two dancers entwined.

His pale blue walls
are not the blue sky of the desert
        at midday sharp as a stiletto
        light cutting eyes
        contrails cutting thin slices of white
out of the sky.
My body is dried ochre
        like linden flowers placed in the sun
        for *tisane* in the winter
when I'd sit with her and wonder
when her bows might untie.

Retreat: A Day on Lama Mountain

I

Mid-morning. The hummingbirds,
out before the sun rose
singing ruby throated songs
flitting from tree to tree
with their unmistakable hum,
have disappeared, and the cicadas
at center stage, their hearts
ignited by the sun's heat
rub their feet together so vigorously
all other sounds fade,
even the chain saws have stopped.
In this non-silence, cicada-song
amplifies into a single white note
a hallucination in the blinding light.

Yesterday I complained of the saws
and compressors, all that energy
bouncing off the bare mountain
bare beneath the dead trees
towering in their charred splendor
remnants of a forest
burned in a tidal wave of fire.
The cicadas hover above the new growth
a river of oaks, oh so many
even the old paths are washed away.
The counterpoint of lush green growth
and stiletto black stalks of Ponderosas
is a cacophony of life and death
broken by a butterfly, a monarch,
yellow and black with elegant flutter
floating in between
the dead branches of the pinons
white calligraphy against the mountain's curve.

II

The sun is high in the not so blue;
over the mountain huge clouds
slate grey, ultramarine purple, lavender
mass together to make mischief.

They come at midday, linger a while
and release pounds of rain, as the airplanes did
after the fire, releasing pounds of seeds
to germinate the mountain floor
    with a rainbow of wildflowers.
The seeds lie in expectant dormancy
longing for rain, wet tenderness
bringing to life its sleeping beauty.
Like her, I sleep in wounded silence
dreaming.

The buzz saw's begun again; a fly's buzz
is deafening and the first crack of thunder
reminds me it's Fourth of July.

III

Yesterday I sat with my old friend
The Healing Tree
her charcoal limbs a black grave
in a grove where thirty years ago
I heard a mantra, a seed song
fruiting finally into soul food, a life of spirit—
not what I studied, nor what I expected;
which is how life works, heading off
in some direction
a chance encounter,
maybe a side path taken,
and what one thought was
is no longer.

I'm waiting for directions.

IV

Late afternoon, impending storm,
and this restless heart
hops from moment to moment
disengaged; even poems pall.
Reading of *eros, agape and philia*
I laugh out loud
alone on a mountaintop, wind picking up,
all around me life in full profusion
as I cultivate boredom as an antidote
to the abundance of life below.
I'd write a love poem
graphic, rich in erotic imagery
but I can't get it up, as they say.
Bored with boredom, with this game
of hide and seek.
When the rain comes
I'll take my clothes off and run outside.
I'll let the cold wet pellets of water
wake me from oblivion.

How many people live like this
all the time?

V

Here on Lama mountain
enshrouded in grey
drops from the sky caress my body
insinuating into each crack and crevice
tickling me.
It doesn't take much.

My husband used to tease that I'd fall in love
with every dog, man, child and tree I met.
These days, I'm a bit more discriminating,
but not much.

VI

When "no" comes,
color and words
offer their beauty
seducing me into form
returning me from chaos.
"Yes" is the acceptance
of meaning.

VII

The rain continues, ground well soaked.
Heaven and Earth embrace,
tendrils of clouds wind their way down
into the dark gash of the Rio Grande Gorge.
In the West the sun sets
brilliant in its dying, the whole sky
filled with creamsicle light,
magenta clouds rest on deep purple peaks.
One final shudder
it's gone.

Fall

In praise of

the calligraphy of roots
the tight compression of energy
a baseball, frayed
skin peeled back, revealing
the skeleton
compassion for the tenderness of paper,
the emptiness of space
black, the collector of color

sacred geometry
sensuous, loping
lines circle in, circle out
a square dance
a tango
mark becomes pattern
pattern becomes grid
image becomes metaphor

the edges permeable

the edge
between structure and chaos—
garden and wilderness
dissolved

simply trust
don't the leaves
flutter down
just like that?

Ghost Ranch

This is where Georgia stood
red rocks scratching the earth,
grey hills sliding into oblivion.

This is where Georgia stood
painting the Pedernal ultramarine
contrasting the turquoise sky, pond
green with algae. Gold

glazes the air under late autumn cottonwoods,
the Chama highlighted by bright red accents
sidewinding its banks.
The Rio del Oso, like the bears in town,
is starving.

Yesterday I stood and looked
at her paintings,
clouds stretching beyond the horizon,
two oak leaves: red-violet and pink,
cerulean sky resting on pelvis.

I yielded to her invitation, seduced
even as those two trees wrapped around each other
held by a fleshy vulva.

In La Cienega

you ask yourself what next,
the slate sky massed with violet clouds.

I call and we walk out of town
chased by a crow, a small white spaniel
teeth bared, squirming through barbed wire
rusty as chamisa in winter.
Two girls, seven and nine, behind
their wrought iron fence run beside us,
a puppy in the younger one's arms.
This is Nickels, he's my new dog—but I want
a kitty. Do you have cats?
      Yes.
Can I have them?
      No;
but if they have kittens (I didn't tell her
they were fixed) I'll bring them by.
Jumping up and down, she and the puppy
squeak. Oh goody! You won't forget?
      No, I won't.

We walk past the ten foot canes
(I cut one into a walking stick),
adobes whitewashed 100 summers,
and follow the etched paths of the land-grant families
looking for *verdolaga* (I call it purslane).
      Years ago in Connecticut I gathered it
        on hot summer days and pickled the fleshy stem
        surprising friends with its dilly-garlic crunch.

At a cattle guard you give me your arm,
my hips slipping in their sockets,
my step unsteady.
        We walked these roads before
        wading into the river over slick rock
        crossing back and forth, drinking beer
        with Juan, almost blind at ninety
        his hands seeing. We walked all day,
        sharp-edged stones hiding carved snakes.
Now there's only an hour or two;
errands need running, lists full of chores,
tonight's my only night home for a week.

We walk back past the two girls behind their fence.
You won't forget?
        No, I won't.

for Elena Montaño

Love creates havoc out of nothing

out of winterfat, branches of white cotton
dabbing at the edges of an empty field

out of a rusted rectangle, its patina
red green blue gold
incongruous desert flower

out of a cat, sunlight streaked belly
exposed in a daring pose
balanced on the wall

out of simple words
liquid
intoxicating the first sip

out of a day's end so still
even havoc is destroyed.

At SITE Santa Fe in November*

Buddha in Blue

Not only your image
but the blue space surrounding you
speaks to this yearning
for wholeness.
That rich cerulean....
I want to eat it
and taste liberation.

Your partner contracted,
a hole in space
—a paradox—
I enter
Alice-like
and fall into licorice darkness.

Objects of Desire

For those who complain
"I don't understand,"
I invite the stillness
of a Sunday afternoon
sitting, watching the way
first color
then image
offer their meaning
to senses worn thin
from an overdosed life.

This yellow
this blue
this holy red
are all the church
I need.

* Based on Sarah Charlesworth's 2-part photograph, *Buddha of Immeasurable Light*

Retreat at Mountain Cloud

In the sacred grove
of play and prayer
I climb the ponderosa
inching up her long, strong arm
extended down
to cover the Earth
with needles so big, so pungent
I feel drunk on her retsina.

Barefoot, my soles are tickled
by her rugged skin offering a toehold
to her next arm, and next;
the branches long gone
now only stumps,
a ladder to Heaven.

As I sit in her arms, ten feet up,
cradled close to her heartwood
two hundred years beating, beating,
all sense of perspective changes;
what this ant mind worried over
scurrying from place to place
disappears. In the canyon
a coyote mother croons a lullaby.

Lament for Rusty

At the market
wood carts filled with the produce
of a plentiful Fall
your eyes full,
wet with a harvest of anguish,
the end of your marriage.

All I could do
was offer a flower,
a lily for the resurrection
that Spring promises.

In the Shadow of the Master

Mastering illusion, I'd slip through time.

I'd enter a Vermeer and let pearl light
bathe my face even as Clio does
holding her trumpet, head triumphant
crowned in laurel, eyes modestly cast down.

I'd sit in the chair at studio's edge
a tapestry rich in reds and ochres
holding us warmly interior.

I'd be a voyeur
watching the master construct space
using pinhole and string,
his ambition: perspective so palpable
we feel his breath, the smell of turpentine.

I'd study the laying down of colored ground,
the sure hand resting lightly on mahlstick,
those active brushstrokes
three hundred years
before de Kooning.

Like an eclipsed moon, I'd be visible
in the light he deflected.

The Magic of Making

The magic of making applesauce
      spluttering on the stove as red leaves
      float one by one on cool currents
      making round scarlet heaps.

The magic of making a poem
      words wandering in and out of line
      locating themselves by surprise.

The magic of making friends
      the alchemy of connection
      bubbling into bonfire.

The magic of making peace
      candlelight casting shadows
      animate in the silence.

The magic of making
      a blank canvas filled,
      layers of color romping
      through forests of calligraphy.

Later, much later
you ask,
who made that?

Weir Farm Fragments

Two huge rocks,
like Buddha
speaking to his disciple,
sunlight splattering
his cloak into a rainbow
of greys.

*

Charter oak
as high as the Empire State
Twin Towers no longer
standing, their lifetime shorter
than expected. This oak
more than 300 years alive.

*

The weather has turned;
large copse of trees
green as summer,
in the center a single red maple
whispering.

*

Old beech
twinned at the hip,
smooth skin
like a clean page,
one sole heart
carved into its flesh.

*

Trees bathed in the golden afternoon,
a squirrel puffs himself up
stealing an acorn
then another
wild dogwood offers its final blaze of red.

*

Bass jumps up
concentric ripples expand
to pond's edge;
surface closes shut
breeze mottling its skin.

*

Squirrel descends
head first with a double acorn
legs splayed, tail puffed,
scolding me between
clenched teeth.

*

In five days
the mushrooms emerged into a cluster,
then rotted—
a heaping black mound.

Calder's Universe

Weighted in a love of material, counterweighted
in the primary colors of my own Crayola childhood
we can talk about his delicacy of balance,
the open space, or quivering line
of piano wire touched by a zephyr,

but I'd rather note how he carved up space, the emptiness
surrounding his floating snowflakes, leaves
and fish swimming in air.

At the Bienecke Library I watched opposing figures
curtsy and bow, do-si-do and allemand left,
then right in the crisp Autumn breeze
moving them in a dance dividing the sky
into circles and squares.

Calder the coyote, dared us to see
what can't be seen
by what can.

Just Before Fall Equinox

A full day of rain,
incessant pattering on the skylights
continual patterning
of drops across windows,
colors greyed.

Each drop holds the smell
of your flesh, fresh and wet
the smell of an after rain:
juniper pungent in nostrils,
fallen leaves rooting into Fall.

When it clears
I'll look up towards the mountains
to see if it's snowed at 10,000 feet.
Have the aspens changed color?
Have they lost their leaves?

Just last week
I sat at the river's orifice
offering prayers to your heart
beating in time with the Earth
the earth scattered with purple asters
and a last red paintbrush
painting the sun red.

Winter

Winter in Tesuque

I am winter,
earth soft
after thaw,
pearlight eyes me.
I shiver, wind
chills bone
breath white
hunched against the cold
juniper smell
held in the glove of my hand
and oh
the Naples yellow
of the grass
pressed down
into pockets
of snow.

Don't Believe Them

They are liars, these
bleak thoughts
icicling your heart.

They are liars, these
doubts scraping
at flesh, crawling into
open wounds depositing
eggs of despair.

They are liars, these
voices
hot, sulfurous whispering:
No good.
Not enough.
Useless.

Living without meaning,
outcast
they struggle to survive
feeding
on lies
believed.

Rousseau's War. 1894

> *It passes by, frightening,*
> *leaving behind despair, tears,*
> *and ruin everywhere.*
> 					—Henri Rousseau

Not the lush jungles I remember from MoMA,
nor the enigmatic gypsy dreaming lion, dreaming
devourer, but another devourer
in a desolate plain like the deserts of Afghanistan,
trees and men broken.

She rides a jet charger, sword and fire in hand,
standing in her stirrups,
lips stretched taut across gritted teeth
crying war, two black holes for eyes.

And what should read fire's destruction
charms by choice of color
peach and ochre clouds in a turquoise sky
contrasting an ebony crow, ripped morsel of flesh
hanging from his bloody beak,
the one spot of red.

The Man from Lodz

On his arm faded numbers in blue
the tattoo of incarceration
only my nightmares remember.
Yet he smiles, this man from Poland
greets us, arms extended
as we enter his studio
Kaddish wailing in the background
a remembrance of the loss
of 6,000,000 and more.
Felix points out the details
of the stained glass model he's made
the Temple at Lodz destroyed in '43.
The parquet floor, well-fitted pieces
of dark and light blue glass,
walls and windows, pews
each remade in miraculous detail.
Here he was to be confirmed.
Instead, his manhood learned
at Dachau.

As a boy in the camps
did he re-count the bricks
to help ease the horror?
Did he silently sing his *Haftorah*
as father
mother
sisters
brothers
uncles
aunts
and friends were killed?
What kept him alive?
What radiance burned through the dark
so that fifty years later
he could rebuild the temple,
the eternal flame glowing red?

Two Poems at Full Moon: New Year, 1999

I   Swathed in luminous scarves
         the full moon appears
         slowly rising above housetops
         where only last week
         Santa with his eight reindeer
         filled the night sky,
         more magic in this round disk
         than any gift that whiskered myth
         could give.

         My womb feels the pull of her tides:
         even now, wrapped
         in her cloudy covering;
         even now without power
         to conceive, this womb pulses
         like a phantom limb.

II   The cats act
         like nothing much
         is happening.
         One cat lifts his leg
         his black paws reaching upward,
         rasp of tongue on fur
         audible in the stillness.
         The other curls her roundness
         onto a cushion molded
         by the warmth of her dreams.

Neither notices
the burlesque of the moon
as she emerges
from gaudy cloudcover.
She bumps and grinds her way
across the sky
shedding her boa and G-string
till the last wisps float away
and nude,
she shines her luminous light
on all three of us;
only I applaud.

Love

Valentine's Day.
To keep my heart happy
I went walking at sunset,
long day lengthening.
In the woods near the river
damp leaves pungent underfoot
my friend Sausage
joined me,
round-bellied, short-legged
floppy-eared
with grizzled beard.
We walked through
red glowing willows
and blazing ochre grasses.
Sausage and I sat
on a haybale bathed in purple
watching the sky show.

Some loves are ecstatic; others
thrive on burgers and fries.

Midwinter

I
Mapping the wild place
travelled only in dark poems
I sweep in truthful circles
far away precincts:
wintry citizens scarved against cold
local stations speak disaster
news of mortality, frozen roots
skulls and broken wings
principles forgotten, faults
no longer distant.

II
Pillowed on iron filings
I lie metallic
eyes pried open
in dreamless sleep
a stumbling flower
cheating this rock heart
of no best friend.
Rose, wiser than a coffin,
you taunt me.

III
Remember the fallen city—
weeping vines, its harbor filled with voyagers
mapping journeys to somewhere?
They inherit a circle of time,
a wanting life.
Unfailing birds sing
perched beside my window
voices soothing wounds
disguised as peace.

Missing Vermeer

In a room somewhere, a painting
is hidden. Unlike the room
in the painting, there is no music.
In a room, a young man masturbates,
a gun at his side.
If he surfed the Web, he'd know
the FBI is handling this case like a kidnapping:
"Our primary concern," they say,
"is the safe recovery of our victim."

In a room in the painting, light
wafts in from the left,
dappling three young people,
a woman singer, a pianist
and a man, sitting straight on a chair
his back to us, playing the lute.
Vermeer was born fifty years before Bach
but I can hear his music.
A cello rests on the diamond patterned floor,
a sharp contrast in black and white
to the figures, held together by an invisible triangle.
I've seen the woman before in other paintings,
lead-tin yellow dress and hair ribbons,
her pearl earrings catching the light.

In my bedroom, a painting
hangs on the wall, the colors strong
discordant. Figures move in different directions
across the landscape washed in red.
Everything is fluid.
At the horizon line, an ultramarine woman
hurries on her way while a triangle, a pyramid
sits at the bottom, a remembrance of Egypt
and other paintings in rooms on walls,
speaking not of space or music
but the importance of kings and queens.
In this room now
Glenn Gould plays the "Goldberg Variations"
and I recognize that I miss Vermeer
the way I miss home
even when I'm here.

("The Concert," a painting by Johannes Vermeer, was stolen from the Isabella Stewart Gardner Museum in Boston in 1990. It is still missing.)

What He Didn't See

My teacher said my painting was primitive,
it had no subtlety, I couldn't draw.
I loved the challenge,
I took his words as a dare.
I spent one year
drawing
drawing
drawing
the fat magnolias filling the studio
with their lush scent,
tables, chairs, stools
boxes, baubles, fat and skinny
models; an old man who posed nude
but wouldn't take his socks off,
my feet are too beat up, he said.
I drew friends, I drew horses
Morgans, muscled, sturdy
a black and white cat marked like a zebra
and red, brown, yellow dogs
long and shorthaired
with names like Salty and Sepia, Xxyzx.
Hands, feet, noses, eyes
eyes in the morning and again late at night.
I drew still lifes alive
with the history of New England
and the wan light of Connecticut winters.
I drew landscapes in the Fall
the Spring, and endless green in Summer.
I looked in the mirror and drew myself
again
and again
and again.
I looked in the mirror and saw I could draw.

February 2nd

February 2nd and Punxsutawney Phil
has peeked around the yard
surprising the taxman.
They eye one another wondering
why they're there.
Phil is out chasing his shadow
wanting to wrap it around him
for the cold to come.
The IRS man is out chasing money
wanting to wrap himself in green
before the Spring thaw.
Neither was invited.

I Didn't Have a *Bas Mitzvah*

for Janet Keller Jurow

I was twelve. Coming home from school I
put on my jeans and a striped T-shirt, the
kind of outfit my mother said, "makes you look
like a lesbian." I didn't
know the word. It was 1957.
Hebrew School began in an hour and I,
only girl in the school, collected my books.
Down the stairs, double-locking the door
I noticed Dad's gingko tree planted
last Spring, frail twig sticking upright. I
wondered if it would survive the winter
as I wondered how the women of my race
survived the prayer recited each morning
by the all-male *minyan* giving thanks
for being made men in God's image,
and not female.

The day was wintry,
a sharp wind from the bay carved
my cheeks. Walking down 212th Street
a figure approached, a dark dot
in an already dark afternoon,
formal topcoat and hat,
the kind my Great Uncle Sam always wore,
sign of an Orthodox Jew.
Rabbi Levine stopped to chat
our teeth chattering in the cold. "Leah,
how are you?" he asked. I answered, "Okay...
thanks...but something's been bugging me."
Saying those words I felt the Red Sea
part inside me and a pathway opened

wide and full of light, the Sea's water
forming huge walls on either side, droplets
of ocean sparkling jewel-like. Dazzled,
not knowing what I'd say
my lips parted and the waters poured forth
steady and strong. "I've decided
not to get *Bas Mitzvahed*. It doesn't feel right;
it's hypocritical.
I don't believe in God.

The boys do it because they're supposed to and
like getting all those presents, all that money.
I can't do it. It's dishonest."

The Rabbi's mouth dropped open, exposing
uneven teeth, yellowed. His eyes looked
pained, bloodshot. "But Leah, you're our star
student! Have you discussed this with your
parents?" "No. This is my decision
and they don't have anything to say
about it." I even surprised myself.

I didn't have a *Bas Mitzvah*.
That day on 212th Street
shivering in the cold, I was confirmed
without ceremony, without gifts.
I found a voice within that was true
and it urged me to listen.
I needed to obey
even at twelve years old,
even if the Rabbi was hurt,
even courting my parents' wrath,
and tempting God's.

Chupadero, January 2000

Frozen river rippled with ice
melting, freezing again;
I pause on a wooden bridge.
Listen: throaty gurgles
amplified by a taut surface.

Yesterday I walked on water.
At the end of the canyon, falls
hidden in the shadows
an icy veil laced with holes
sun-thawed at midday.

Returning, I slipped
a glassy patch
catching me as I turned
to watch a bluebird—
laughter as red as my jacket.

Black Painting

Before creation
black. Black as the caverns
    at Carlsbad
    before their discovery.
Black as the new moon. Black
as a black hole sucking the sky
empty. Seven feet long of black:
    jet, ebony, ink,
    lampblack, blueblack, coal.

Closer it fractures.
This one large mass holds the full spectrum
embedded in its layers
crimson scumbled
across the top
like dropped leaves in fall.

The textured surface cut,
scraped, sanded away
exposing a lapis
worth more than gold.
Hints of yellow skip across
the picture plane; hansa, azo, cadmium.
A glaze of Hooker's green. In the lower left
lavender smelling of Provence;
    umber, ochre and sienna,
    Tuscan hills at sunrise.

Faint shapes scratch into the pitch:
    Cambrian corals,
    a fish, a brontosaurus
    a garden of ocean flowers waving.
The first man steps into Eden, naked.

A sonnet of light.

The dark shudders, shatters
    crystalline slivers
    chant
the thousand and one names.

Spring, again

What do you plan to do?

What do you plan to do with your one wild and precious life?
                              Mary Oliver

I will paint myself cobalt
and soar with the bluebirds
             deepening the color of the midday sky.

I'll cloak myself in cactus flowers
tango on a mesa with the moon in my arms
             a necklace of stars haunting my throat.

I'll chase dolphins towards Atlantis
buried deep in turquoise waters
             riotous somersaults, joyous leaps.

I'll do all the doing
until the doing is done
             then be still as Kailas mountain.

I'll lay down in my garden
grapes and apple trees
             cats and poems a bower.

I'll do all the doing
until the doing is done
             and sleep wrapped in the Perseids.

I'll rest my head on indigo night
and dream songs etched in gold
             seducing the wilderness of dawn.

Acknowledgments

Many thanks to Robert French and Jay Udall for their care and thoughtfulness as editors, to Pat Shapiro for her helpful reading of the manuscript, and to Markanthony Felix for his computer expertise.

The following poems first appeared in these publications:

"About Silence"
> in *Insight*

"I Didn't Have A *Bas Mitzvah*" (Previously titled "Coming of Age")
> in *Jewish Women's Literary Annual (Volume 5)*

"In Memoriam"
> in *CC: Connecticut College Magazine*

"Retreat: A Day on Lama Mountain"
> was originally made as an Artist's Book and then published in *Santa Fe Poetry Broadside* and *Just Outside the Frame*

"Retreat at Mountain Cloud"
> in *Dharma Mirror*

"Sunday Morning Early"
> in *Clackamas Literary Review*

"Winter in Tesuque"
> in *Women Becoming Poems*

"Weir Farm Fragments"
> was originally made as a limited edition Artist's Book while I was Artist-in-Residence at Weir Farm National Historic Site in Wilton, CT.

"Woman in Yellow"
> in *Borderlands: Texas Poetry Review*

This book of poetry has been printed on acid-free paper.
The typeface is Palatino.

www.ingramcontent.com/pod-product-compliance
Lightning Source LLC
Chambersburg PA
CBHW021021090426
42738CB00007B/856